POP CULTURE BIOS

ROSS

LYNCH

ACTOR, SINGER, DANCER, SUPERSTAR

HEATHER E. SCHWARTZ

D0856490

Lerner Publications
MINNEAPOLI

Lerner Publications Company
A division of Lerner Publishing Group, Inc.
241 First Avenue North
Minneapolis, MN 55401 USA

For reading levels and more information, look up this title at
www.lernerbooks.com.

Library of Congress Cataloging-in-Publication Data

Schwartz, Heather E., author.
        Ross Lynch : actor, singer, dancer, superstar / by Heather
    E. Schwartz.
            pages   cm. — (Pop culture bios)
        Includes index.
        ISBN 978-1-4677-3671-8 (lib. bdg. : alk. paper)
        ISBN 978-1-4677-4734-9 (eBook)
        1. Lynch, Ross, 1995– 2. Rock musicians—United States—
    Biography. I. Title.
    ML420.L943S38 2015
    782.42164092—dc23 [B]   2013048312

Manufactured in the United States of America
1 – PC – 7/15/14

INTRODUCTION

Fans screamed and leapt from their seats to cheer for the star of the moment: Ross Lynch. He'd just been named the winner of Video VIP: Best Music Video at the 2013 Radio Disney Music Awards. So was the seventeen-year-old star screaming too? Nah. Ross was cool as a cucumber— but that didn't mean he wasn't super stoked.

Ross poses with his Radio Disney Music Award.

Ross jumped up, showing off his white skinny jeans and black leather jacket. As he made his way onstage, he slapped fans' hands while his winning song, "Heard It on the Radio," played in the background. Once there, he knelt like a knight in shining armor to humbly accept his gold trophy.

Maia Mitchell (CENTER) and Ross Lynch (RIGHT) answer interview questions during the Radio Disney Music Awards.

As he spoke from the stage, his excitement came through in his voice. **"Wow, this is really, really cool,"** he said. "Thanks, guys!" Before leaving the stage, he thanked the fans of R5, the band he performed in with his siblings and best friend. And afterward, he told a reporter that winning felt "incredible."

It was just one of many incredible moments in Ross's life so far.

CHAPTER ONE

RISING STAR

Ross (CENTER), his sibs, and family friend Ellington Ratliff (LEFT) goof around at the Empire State Building.

Once upon a time, the swoon-worthy Ross Shor Lynch was just a regular little kid. Born on December 29, 1995, he grew up in Littleton, Colorado. Like other kids, he went to school and thought singing and dancing were fun hobbies. Ross and his siblings had a checkered dance floor in their basement. It was perfect for jamming to tunes by Michael Jackson, Bruce Springsteen, the Backstreet Boys, and *NSYNC. He and his siblings loved putting on shows for their parents and relatives.

Ross grew up in Littleton, Colorado.

It wasn't long before someone recognized their gifts. Who was that talent scout? Their mom, of course! She saw her kids had skills and put them in dance lessons so they could improve their moves. With some professional polish, maybe—just maybe—the Lynch gang could take their talents from cellar to center stage.

Ross is a cousin of professional dancers Julianne and Derek Hough. But they didn't play a role in his rise to stardom. Ross earned his fame through toil and talent.

Ross (SECOND FROM LEFT) with siblings and friend Ellington Ratliff (CENTER)

Leaving Littleton

Ross started his dance training in 2001. Soon he was teaching himself to play guitar too. He was really busy and super focused on music and dancing. So from fourth grade on, he was homeschooled.

LAST DAY OF SCHOOL

One year, Ross's class took a trip to the park. Even after he became a superstar, he never forgot how much fun he had kicking off summer with snacks and sports. It was the greatest last day of school he ever had!

He wasn't the only rising star in the family. When Ross was eleven, his oldest brother, Riker, was ready to make a move—to Hollywood. He wanted to break into showbiz, and his family was ready to back him up. In 2007, the Lynches left Littleton for a new life in Los Angeles, California.

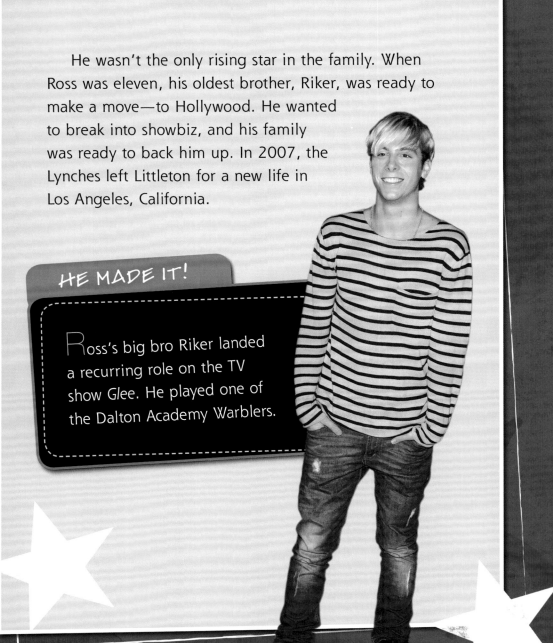

HE MADE IT!

Ross's big bro Riker landed a recurring role on the TV show *Glee*. He played one of the Dalton Academy Warblers.

In 2009, Ross worked alongside Moises Arias (RIGHT) on the TV show *Moises Rules!*

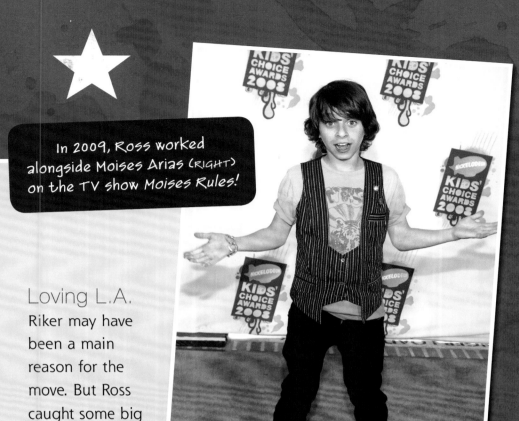

Loving L.A.

Riker may have been a main reason for the move. But Ross caught some big breaks of his own in L.A. In 2009, he joined the pop group Kidz Bop Kids and sang on *Kidz Bop 15*. He also danced in the group Rage Boyz Crew. That same year, Ross also made an appearance on the TV show *Moises Rules!* In 2010, he had a part in the movie *Grapple!*

> **EP =**
>
> _a musical recording that includes more songs than a single but fewer than a full-length album. EP is short for extended play._

Ross wasn't just making a splash in his solo career. He also sang lead vocals and played guitar in the band R5. It was a family act. The band includes brothers Riker on bass and Rocky on guitar. Ross's sister, Rydel, plays keyboards. The final band member (and the fifth _R_ in R5) is Ellington Ratliff, who plays drums. In 2009, R5 released its first EP, _Ready Set Rock_.

Members of R5 (LEFT TO RIGHT) Ellington Ratliff, Rydel Lynch, Rocky Lynch, Ross Lynch, and Riker Lynch

Ross didn't need to worry about his career as a performer. He was already having major success. And he was about to get his biggest break yet.

ANOTHER BROTHER

Ross also has a brother named Ryland. While he's talented too, he's not a member of R5. Instead, he acts as the band's manager.

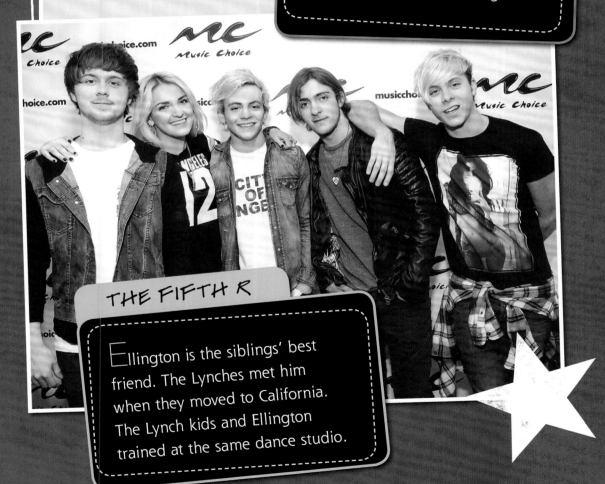

THE FIFTH R

Ellington is the siblings' best friend. The Lynches met him when they moved to California. The Lynch kids and Ellington trained at the same dance studio.

CHAPTER TWO

LEADING MAN

Ross performing at a Christmas tree lighting ceremony in California in 2009.

LEAD =
the main role in a show

While his band was getting off the ground, Ross auditioned for a new Disney show called *Austin & Ally*. Out of all the hopeful actors, he quickly rose to the top. Why wouldn't he? The show needed a male lead who could do it all: sing, dance, and act.

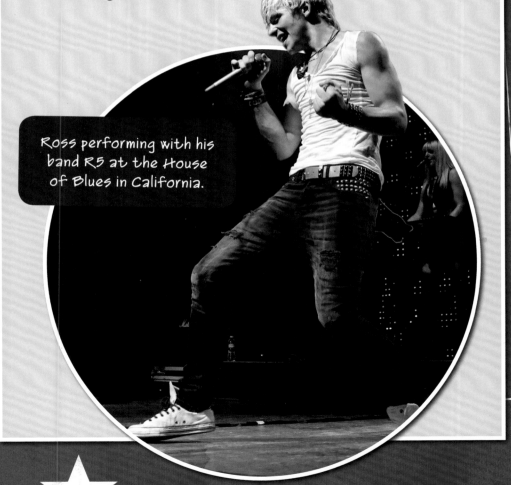

Ross performing with his band R5 at the House of Blues in California.

As the front man for R5, Ross had the first talent covered. He'd mastered the second skill after years of dance classes and training. He'd also honed his acting chops by appearing in about twenty national commercials. The role of Austin Moon had Ross written all over it. And by early 2011, he was on set starring opposite actress Laura Marano.

FRONT MAN =
the main performer in a band

ROSS AND LAURA

Ross has said he and *Austin & Ally* costar Laura Marano act like a married couple on set. They sometimes bicker, but they always have each other's backs.

Old School

The Beatles
Bruce Springsteen
Elvis
Led Zeppelin
The Rolling Stones

New School

Bruno Mars
John Mayer

Austin & Ally was much more than an acting gig for Ross. He sang the show's theme song, "Can't Do It without You," and as Austin, he performed songs throughout the show. They were compiled on the *Austin & Ally* sound track—a huge hit that reached No. 1 on *Billboard*'s sound tracks chart in September 2012. Beginner's luck? Not a chance! **"He's a talented singer and one of the hardest working guys I know,"** said Ben Charles, the sound track's producer.

Ross rocks out while filming an episode of *Austin & Ally*.

19

Ross has said he would love to take a girl surfing or skydiving on a date.

We <3 Ross

With his blond locks and supersweet smile, Ross shot to heartthrob status in no time. He was in high demand for photo shoots. Websites posted videos of him dancing and doing flips on the beach. Radio Disney ran a contest giving fans the chance to meet Ross. And he won a Battle of the Blond Heartthrobs contest on Teen.com.

He was the country's hottest new crush. But he hadn't actually asked out any crushes of his own yet. Why the wait? It could be he was too busy to date. After all, he wasn't *just* the star of a Disney series. He was also still very involved with his band, R5.

Ross chats with excited fans.

Lead Singer

In April 2012, R5 signed with Hollywood Records. The next month, Ross and his bandmates hit the road on a West Coast tour. On top of that, the band had new music to record. In February 2013, they put out the four-song EP *Loud*. They also made a music video for the song "Loud" from the album.

Ross performing with R5 at the 2012 Magnificent Mile Lights Festival in Chicago.

As if all that weren't enough, Ross found time for yet another project. He was starring in the made-for-TV Disney film *Teen Beach Movie*. Many days, his schedule was packed from morning to night. He filmed *Austin & Ally* during the day and rehearsed with R5 until ten or eleven at night. He had plenty of priorities to juggle. And he wasn't about to slow down!

STRATEGIES FOR STRESS

With a jam-packed schedule, Ross is bound to get stressed once in a while. He tames the tension by listening to music, playing music, or reading a good book.

Cast members from *Teen Beach Movie* have a blast at the Disney Parks Christmas Day Parade in California!

CHAPTER THREE

MOVIES, MUSIC, AND MORE

Ross on set with costar Maia Mitchell

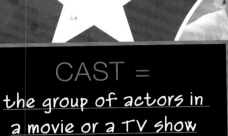

CAST =
the group of actors in
a movie or a TV show

Filming *Teen Beach Movie* was super fun. To film those great beach scenes, Ross traveled to Puerto Rico. He loved getting a close-up look at Puerto Rican culture. But dancing in the sand for hours wasn't as easy as fans might have thought. It got scorchingly hot! Ross and the rest of the cast had to hydrate with plenty of water.

FILM FAV

Ross loved performing his singing and dance scenes in *Teen Beach Movie*. But his favorite scene to film was a different challenge altogether. It was an emotional moment with onscreen girlfriend McKenzie (played by Maia Mitchell). Aw!

Still, Ross enjoyed life by the sea and had no complaints. To relax during their time off, he and his cast pals had loads of options. They swam in the always warm water. They played music together on the beach in the middle of the night. And they even had a close encounter with a shark while snorkeling. It wasn't exactly relaxing, but the adventure brought them closer together. They held onto one another for dear life!

Ross has a whole collection of skinny jeans. He has them in green, blue, hot pink, and even patterns.

Ross riding up in style to the *Teen Beach Movie* premiere in Australia

Winning Performances

Ross's accomplishments didn't go unnoticed. For one thing, he won some major awards. He was voted Favorite TV Actor at the 2013 Kids' Choice Awards. The same year, he won the Radio Disney Music Award for Video VIP: Best Music Video for his song "Heard It on the Radio" from the *Austin & Ally* sound track.

SOCIAL MEDIA HOUND

Ross spends a lot of time on social media, especially Twitter and Instagram. He says it's a great way to connect with fans.

Not only that, he scored more acting roles too. In *Muppets Most Wanted*, he joined a cast that included major stars, from Lady Gaga to Tina Fey. He also did his first voice-over work, playing Jack Russell, or Werewolf by Night, on an episode of *Ultimate Spider-Man*. Working with a mic was nothing new for Ross, since he was so used to singing. But voicing an animated character was definitely different. For one thing, he had to brush up on his growl!

VOICE-OVER = words spoken in a movie or a TV show by a person who is not seen

Ross poses at the premiere of *Muppets Most Wanted.*

R5 performs in New York.

Face Forward

Through it all, Ross remained dedicated to R5. In September 2013, the band released its debut full-length album, *Louder*. It landed in the top 30 on the *Billboard* 200 chart. A *Louder* world tour was planned for 2014.

For Ross, it was just the beginning. He told reporters he hopes the band will still be playing together in ten years. Maybe by then, they'll be putting out their sixth album and heading out for another world tour.

DEBUT =
first album or performance for the public

As for his acting career, Ross doesn't plan to give that up anytime soon either. He hopes for bigger movies and bigger roles. He's a hardworking star with tons of talent. All of his goals are within his grasp.

ROSS
PICS!

Ross and Maia Mitchell

Ross and Laura Marano

R5 performs in London in 2014

29

SOURCE NOTES

7   "Ross Lynch Wins Best Music Video RDMAS," YouTube video, 0:32, posted by "Ross Lynch," May 4, 2013, http://www.youtube.com/watch?v=_rcZtG4LFr0.

7   Ibid.

19 "On the Charts: Ben Charles on the *Austin & Ally* Soundtrack," *American Society of Composers, Authors and Publishers*, October 3, 2012, http://www.ascap.com /playback/2012/10/wecreatemusic/ben-charles.aspx.

MORE ROSS INFO

BOP & Tiger Beat Online: Ross Lynch
http://www.bopandtigerbeat.com/tag/ross-lynch
Get the dish with stories, photos, and videos of Ross Lynch from this celeb mag.

R5 Official Site
https://www.r5rocks.com/home
Learn more about Ross's band on their official website.

R5's Facebook Page
https://www.facebook.com/officialR5
Track R5's upcoming gigs and check out photos of the band.

Ross's Facebook Page
https://www.facebook.com/RossR5
If you're a Facebook user, join the millions of fans who "Like" this page. While you're there, check out status updates and photos.

Ross's Instagram Page
http://web.stagram.com/n/rossr5
Check out Ross's latest pics.

Ross's Twitter Page
https://twitter.com/rossR5
Get up-to-the-minute updates from Ross himself.

INDEX

The images in this book are used with the permission of: © Chelsea Lauren/Getty Images, pp. 3, (top), 11, 16 (bottom left), ; © Ben Horton/WireImage/Getty Images, pp. 3 (bottom), 22 (bottom left); © Michael N. Todaro/Getty Images, p. 4 (upper right); © Michael Schwartz/WireImages/Getty Images, p. 4 (bottom); © Ilya Savenok/Getty Images, pp. 4 (upper left), 12, 16 (top); © Frederick M. Brown/Getty Images, p. 6; © Rachel Murray/Getty Images, p. 7; © Cindy Ord/Getty Images, p. 8 (upper left); © Rahav Segev/WireImage/Getty Images, p. 8 (bottom); © Steve Granitz/WireImage /Getty Images, pp. 8 (upper right), 26; © Hyoung Chang/Denver Post/Getty Images, p. 9; © Jun Sato/WireImage/Getty Images, p. 10; © Alberto E. Rodriguez/Getty Images, p. 13; © Barry Brecheisen/WireImage/Getty Images, p. 14; © Astrid Starwairz/agency/Getty Images, p. 15; © Jo Hale/Getty Images, p. 16 (bottom right); © Paul Archuleta/FilmMagic/Getty Images, pp. 17, 22 (bottom right), 28 (bottom right), 29 (top middle); © Eric McCandless/Disney ABC Television Group/Getty Images, pp. 18, 19 © Don Arnold/WireImage/Getty Images, p. 20; © Timothy Hiatt/ Getty Images, p. 21; © Handout/Getty Images, p. 22 (top); © Francisco Roman/Disney ABC Television Group/Getty Images, p. 23; © Bob D'Amico/Disney ABC Television Group/Getty Images, p. 24; © Brendon Thorne/Getty Images, p. 25; © Rob Kim/Getty Images, p. 27; © Don Arnold/ WireImage/Getty Images, p. 28 (left); © Bruce Glikas/FilmMagic/Getty Images, p. 28 (top right); © Jo Hale/Redferns/Getty Images, p. 29 (bottom); © Mark Davis/KCA2014/Getty Images, p. 29 (top left); © Rob Kim/FilmMagic/Getty Images, p. 29 (top right).

Front Cover: © FeatureFlash/Shutterstock.com (large image); © Jo Hale/Redferns/Getty Images (inset).
Back Cover: © Rodrigo Vaz/FilmMagic/Getty Images.

Main body text set in Shannon Std Book 12/18.
Typeface provided by Monotype Typography.